SHE'S GOT GAME
WOMEN IN SOCCER

by Donna B. McKinney

FOCUS
READERS.
NAVIGATOR

WWW.FOCUSREADERS.COM

Focus Readers is distributed by North Star Editions:
sales@northstareditions.com | 888-417-0195

Produced for Focus Readers by Red Line Editorial.

Photographs ©: Tony Gutierrez/AP Images, cover, 1; Mike Blake/Reuters/Newscom, 4–5; Rose Prouser/Reuters/Newscom, 7; Gary Hershorn/Reuters/Newscom, 9; The Picture Art Collection/Alamy, 10–11; History and Art Collection/Alamy, 13; Herbert French/National Photo Company Collection/Library of Congress, 15; Aspen Photo/Shutterstock Images, 16–17; Chen guo/Imaginechina/AP Images, 19; Jose Manuel Ribeiro/Reuters/Newscom, 21; Bob Tringali/SportsChrome/Newscom, 23; Oleksandr Osipov/Shutterstock Images, 24–25; feelphoto/Shutterstock Images, 27; lev radin/Shutterstock Images, 29

Library of Congress Cataloging-in-Publication Data
Library of Congress Cataloging-in-Publication Data is available on the Library of Congress website.

ISBN
978-1-64493-062-5 (hardcover)
978-1-64493-141-7 (paperback)
978-1-64493-299-5 (ebook pdf)
978-1-64493-220-9 (hosted ebook)

Printed in the United States of America
Mankato, MN
012020

ABOUT THE AUTHOR

Donna B. McKinney is a writer who lives in North Carolina. She spent many years writing about science and technology topics at the US Naval Research Laboratory in Washington, DC. Now she enjoys writing about topics ranging from science to history to sports for children and young adults.

TABLE OF CONTENTS

CHAPTER 1

SHOOTOUT AT THE WORLD CUP

In 1999, two soccer teams met in Pasadena, California, for the Women's World Cup finals. At the end of two hours of play, the United States and China were tied 0–0. The match went to a shootout. Players from both teams would take turns shooting the ball. Only the goalie would be allowed to defend the goal.

At the 1999 World Cup, US player Kristine Lilly competes with China's Liu Ailing.

Some critics had questioned whether fans would watch women's soccer. But the fans showed up. Approximately 90,000 people attended the game between the United States and China. That crowd was the largest ever for a women's soccer game. Another 40 million people watched the game live on TV.

The US team featured players known as the Fab Five. These players were Mia Hamm, Joy Fawcett, Kristine Lilly, Brandi Chastain, and Julie Foudy. Each member of the Fab Five had been on the team for more than 10 years. Some of them had been high school sophomores when they joined the team.

The 1999 Women's World Cup took place at a sold-out Rose Bowl in Pasadena, California.

To reach the finals, the United States and China had defeated some great teams. In the semifinals, the US team beat Brazil. China beat Norway. Both of those games were hard fought.

Now, a shootout was going to decide the World Cup champion.

Soon, the shootout was tied 4–4. If the US team scored its next shot, it would win the World Cup. The US coach chose Chastain to take the shot. Chastain could shoot well with either foot. This time, she used her left foot to drive the ball toward the goal. The ball soared past the Chinese goalie and into the net. The US team had won the Women's World Cup!

The Fab Five were winners for many years. They won two Women's World Cups. They also won two Olympic gold medals. Women had been playing soccer for more than 100 years. But the success

Brandi Chastain watches her shot go into the net to win the 1999 Women's World Cup.

of the 1999 US team helped inspire many young girls to play soccer. The future looked bright for women's soccer around the world.

CHAPTER 2

EARLY YEARS

People have been playing games similar to soccer for thousands of years. In the 300s BCE, people in China began playing a game known as Cuju. Players used a leather ball filled with feathers. They tried to get the ball into a net using their feet and bodies. They did not use their hands.

A painting from the 1300s shows a Chinese emperor and others playing Cuju.

Modern soccer developed in the United Kingdom in 1863. Women's soccer started to become popular soon after. In 1881, women's teams from Scotland and England played a game against one another. The women played in stockings and high-heeled boots. A newspaper reported that the game ended when people chased the women off the field.

By 1894, women were playing in soccer shoes instead of high heels. The next year, Nettie Honeyball helped form the British Ladies' Football Club. Honeyball was a well-known soccer player. She wanted to show that women were capable in ways that some men thought they

The first British women's soccer team was formed in Edinburgh, Scotland, in the late 1800s.

were not. Approximately 10,000 people watched the club's first match.

During World War I (1914–1918), millions of British men fought in Europe. British women took on new roles at home. As a result, women's soccer grew. The sport drew large crowds during this time.

Lily Parr was one of the game's most famous players. One of Parr's teammates said she could kick like a mule. She scored nearly 1,000 goals during her career.

When World War I ended, some people wanted to return to **traditional** ways. Many thought that women were not

LILY PARR

Lily Parr began playing on a soccer team in 1919. She was 14 years old. Parr scored 43 goals that first season. Her soccer career lasted for more than 30 years, until 1951. Parr was also openly gay during her life. During that time, many gay women hid their sexuality. Parr was fearless on and off the field.

In the early 1900s, some US women played soccer. But organized US soccer for women occurred much later.

supposed to play soccer. In 1921, the United Kingdom banned women's soccer. In response, some British players went to the United States to play. And women still played soccer in Italy, France, Norway, and Germany.

CHAPTER 3

THE SOCCER BOOM

For decades, women's soccer was less popular in the United States than it was in other countries. But in 1972, Title IX became law in the United States. This law requires US colleges to give **proportional** funding to female and male athletes. As a result, colleges started offering athletic **scholarships** to women.

College soccer players compete for the ball.

By 1981, nearly 100 US colleges had women's **varsity** soccer teams.

Title IX supported a new generation of soccer stars. Michelle Akers was one of these players. In 1984, Akers received a scholarship at the University of Central

THE GODMOTHER OF TITLE IX

In 1969, Bernice Sandler was applying to become a college teacher. But colleges kept turning her down. She realized she was being turned down because she was a woman. In response, Sandler studied gender **discrimination** at colleges across the United States. Then she worked with a lawmaker to fix the problem. In 1972, that lawmaker helped pass Title IX. Because of her work, Sandler is often called the Godmother of Title IX.

Michelle Akers shoots against Brazil during the 1991 Women's World Cup.

Florida. In 1985, she joined the first US Women's National Team. This team played in **FIFA**'s first Women's World Cup in 1991. In the final game, Akers scored the winning goal for the United States.

That same year, Akers learned she had chronic fatigue syndrome. This illness causes extreme tiredness. And exercise often makes the illness feel worse. But Akers was set on continuing her soccer career.

Akers played on the 1996 US Olympic team. That year, women's soccer was part of the Olympics for the first time. Men's soccer had been an Olympic event for nearly 100 years. The US women's team won the gold medal. However, the game was not shown on TV.

The 1999 Women's World Cup was shown on TV in the United States. And for the first time, the games were played

Sun Wen pushes forward with the ball during a
1999 match against the United States.

in large stadiums. That year, Sun Wen of
China won the Golden Ball award. This
prize is given to the best player in the
World Cup. The 1999 tournament brought
women's soccer to new heights around
the world.

MIA HAMM

Mia Hamm was born in Alabama in 1972. At 15 years old, Hamm joined the US Women's National Team. In 1989, she received a scholarship to play at the University of North Carolina. Hamm led the team to four college titles.

In 1991, Hamm helped the US team win the first Women's World Cup. In 1999, the team won another World Cup. She led the US team to two Olympic gold medals as well. FIFA twice named Hamm the world's best female player.

Hamm was a top-scoring **forward**. She could drive through nearly any team's defense. She scored a record-setting 158 goals in international games. Many fans agree that Hamm was one of the greatest female athletes ever.

Mia Hamm dribbles down the field during a 1998 match for Team USA.

CHAPTER 4

GOING PRO

Many of the world's best female soccer players play for professional teams. One of the most popular leagues is in France. This league started in 1975. As of 2018, an average of approximately 21,000 fans attended each game.

The National Women's Soccer League (NWSL) is the professional US league.

Ada Hegerberg lands a header during a game for Lyon of the French League Division 1 Féminine.

The first NWSL games took place in 2013. The NWSL is the country's third women's pro league. The first two leagues lasted only a few seasons.

Alex Morgan joined the NWSL in its first season. In 2013, she helped the Portland Thorns win the league's first

THE 2019 WORLD CUP

In 2019, 24 national teams faced off in France for the Women's World Cup. The US team was the defending champion. Alex Morgan and Megan Rapinoe led the team's charge. They each scored six goals in the tournament. They helped the United States beat the Netherlands in the final to win gold. Rapinoe won the Golden Boot and the Golden Ball.

Alex Morgan launches the ball during a 2019 Women's World Cup game against Thailand.

championship. Morgan has also led the US Women's National Team. In 2012, the team won the Olympic gold medal. In 2015 and 2019, Morgan led the team to two straight Women's World Cups.

In 2017, Marta Vieira da Silva also began playing for the NWSL. She joined the Orlando Pride. Growing up in Brazil, Marta faced barriers to playing soccer. From 1941 until 1979, Brazil banned girls and women from playing the game. However, Marta did not let those **prejudices** slow her career. In 2018, FIFA named her the best women's player in the world. That was Marta's sixth time winning that award. As of 2019, she held the record for most goals in the Women's World Cup.

Stars like Marta and Morgan continue to inspire more and more female soccer players. As of 2018, approximately

Marta (left) makes a move during a 2018 game against Japan.

30 million girls and women played soccer around the world. Looking ahead, new stars are sure to keep women's soccer growing.

FOCUS ON
WOMEN IN SOCCER

Write your answers on a separate piece of paper.

1. Write a paragraph that describes how Title IX affected women's soccer.

2. Which women's soccer player would you most like to watch? Why?

3. How many goals did Lily Parr score during her career?

    A. nearly 150 goals
    B. nearly 500 goals
    C. nearly 1,000 goals

4. Why did women's soccer become popular in the United Kingdom during World War I?

    A. Fewer men were at home to play soccer.
    B. Women learned about soccer from soldiers in Europe.
    C. Men's soccer was banned during the war.

Answer key on page 32.

GLOSSARY

discrimination
Unfair treatment of others based on who they are or how they look.

FIFA
Short for Fédération Internationale de Football Association, an international soccer organization.

forward
An offensive position that is usually played by a quick player who is a strong shooter.

prejudices
Unfair judgments of others based on who they are or how they look.

proportional
Having numbers or amounts that have the same relationship between one another.

scholarships
Money given to students to pay for education expenses.

traditional
Following practices that have been common in the past.

varsity
The top team representing a high school or college in a sport or competition.

TO LEARN MORE

BOOKS

Carothers, Thomas. *Women's World Cup Heroes.* Minneapolis: Abdo Publishing, 2019.

Doeden, Matt. *More Than a Game: Race, Gender, and Politics in Sports.* Minneapolis: Lerner Publishing Group, 2020.

Scheff, Matt. *Alex Morgan: Soccer Star.* Lake Elmo, MN: Focus Readers, 2019.

NOTE TO EDUCATORS

Visit **www.focusreaders.com** to find lesson plans, activities, links, and other resources related to this title.

INDEX